Know It All!
Beginner Guides to the Big World

Let's Learn All About Science!

WINDMILL BOOKS

Published in 2025 by Windmill Books,
an Imprint of Rosen Publishing
2544 Clinton St.
Buffalo, NY 14224

Publishing Director Belinda Gallagher
Creative Director Jo Cowan
Editorial Director Rosie Neave
Senior Editor Sarah Carpenter
Senior Designers Emily Stalley, Joe Jones
Image Manager Liberty Newton
Production Elizabeth Collins
Reprographics Stephan Davis
Assets Venita Kidwai
Consultant Barbara Taylor

Cataloging-in-Publication Data

Names: Woolf, Alex, 1964-, author. | Potter, Alice, illustrator.
Title: Let's learn all about science! / by Alex Woolf, illustrated by Alice Potter.
Description: Buffalo, New York : Windmill Books, 2025. | Series: Know it all!: beginner guides to the big world
Identifiers: ISBN 9781538395950 (pbk.) | ISBN 9781538395967 (library bound) | ISBN 9781538395974 (ebook)
Subjects: LCSH: Science--Juvenile literature.
Classification: LCC Q163.W78 2025 | DDC 500--dc23

Printed in the United States of America
CPSIA Compliance Information: Batch #CSWM25: For Further Information contact Rosen Publishing at 1-800-237-9932

Know It All!

Beginner Guides to the Big World

Let's Learn All About Science!

Alex Woolf

Illustrated by Alice Potter

WINDMILL BOOKS

Contents

There are so many cool science facts to discover in this book. Weeeee!

What is science?

Science is all about being curious and asking questions. Scientists are people whose job it is to observe the world around them. They want to find out how and why things happen.

There are many different types of sciences, such as botany, astronomy, and geology.

Collecting data

Scientists collect data, or information. They measure, weigh, and record the speeds of lots of things, from animals to machinery.

Scientists explore the world to try and understand it. They often use devices to help them, like this microscope.

Scientific method

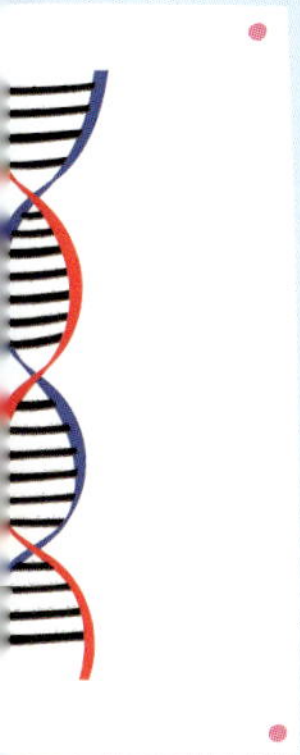

1 Ask a QUESTION such as: If I use heavier paper, will my paper plane fly further?

2 Think what the answer could be – that is your THEORY.

3 Carry out an EXPERIMENT to test your theory.

4 Record the results and come to a CONCLUSION.

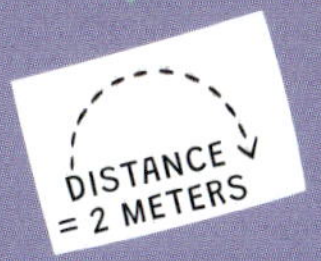

How does it work?

Some things, like magnets and rainbows, seem like magic. But scientists want to know how they work.

I CAN... MEASURE MYSELF

Collect some data about yourself. How tall are you? How long is your arm and your foot? Write down your guesses, then use a tape measure to measure yourself. How accurate were your guesses?

Living Earth

Life can be found almost everywhere on Earth, from deserts to polar lands, and from mountaintops to the deepest oceans.

Living things need **food** for energy.

Macaw

Sloth

Plants move their leaves to reach sunlight.

They **excrete waste** products.

What is life?

A living thing is anything that can move, feel, breathe, eat, excrete, grow, and reproduce.

Scientists who study life are called biologists.

Insects

I CAN... TELL LIVING FROM NONLIVING

Have a look around you. Write a list of some living and nonliving things you can see. Think about what makes them different from each other.

Living things can **move** using their own energy.

All living things **breathe**. They breathe in oxygen and breathe out carbon dioxide.

Living things make new body parts and change old or damaged ones. A caterpillar **changes** into a butterfly, and a tree grows new branches.

All life-forms can **feel** if something touches them, or if there's a change in the atmosphere.

All living things **reproduce** (create offspring). Most animals need a partner to reproduce.

A cockroach can live for up to one week without its head!

Discovering plants

From giant oak trees to tiny buttercups, plants can be all shapes and sizes. They take water and carbon dioxide from the air and turn them into food using the energy in sunlight.

Bees carry pollen from flower to flower.

See you, seed!

Plant seeds go on a journey so the young plant can grow somewhere else. They may be blown on the wind, carried by water, or spread by animals.

Most plants **reproduce** (make young plants) when pollen from the male part of one flower travels to the female part of another flower, and creates a seed.

The **leaves** capture energy from sunlight. A chemical in the leaves stores this energy.

Fruit

Some plants surround their seeds with tasty fruit. An animal eats the fruit, and the seeds come out in their poop, ready to grow in a new place.

I CAN... SEE IF PLANTS NEED LIGHT

Fill two containers with soil and plant a basil, mint, or thyme seed in each one. Place one by the window and another in the shade. Spray with water each day. Which one grows best, and why?

The **roots** draw in minerals and water, which the plant needs to live and grow. Roots also keep the plant stable and upright.

Sunflower seeds

The animal world

Animals can be big or tiny. Some fly, some hop, some crawl and some swim. They may have no legs, two, four, six, or eight legs, and be covered in skin, feathers, fur, or scales.

Most of the animals on Earth (97 percent) are invertebrates.

Which group?

Animals are divided into six main groups. Five of the groups are vertebrates (have a backbone). Invertebrates, which include insects, have no backbone.

Food chains

All living things need food. Plants make their food from sunlight, water, and air. Animals, such as mice, eat plants for food. Mice are food for snakes, and snakes are food for eagles. This is called a food chain.

I CAN... MAKE A BIRD FEEDER

Ask an adult to help. Make lots of small holes in a plastic bottle with scissors. Fill with bird seed. Push pencils through the bottom holes. Add a hole to the lid, thread in string then knot. Do up the lid and hang the feeder outside.

Life cycles

The journey of a living thing from birth to death is called its life cycle. In some species, the young look very different from the adults. Butterflies begin life as caterpillars, and frogs begin as tadpoles.

Habitats

A habitat is the natural home of a plant or animal. Habitats may be cold or hot, wet or dry, on land or in the ocean. Living things adapt to survive in their habitats.

Polar regions

These cold, windy places have lots of snow and ice. Trees cannot grow here, but some plants can. Polar animals, such as **polar bears** and **penguins**, have thick fur or feathers.

Deserts

These places are very dry, and can be hot or cold. **Camels** can go without water for over a week. They have wide feet so they don't sink in the sand.

Some areas in the Atacama Desert in Chile have not had rain for over 500 years!

Rainforests

These warm, wet places are full of trees and plants. Most animals, such as **toucans**, live in the canopy, a thick layer of branches and leaves at the tops of the trees.

I CAN... SEARCH FOR INSECTS

Parks and gardens are excellent microhabitats. You will find insects flying through the air, feasting on plants, and hiding under rocks and stones. See how many different kinds you can spot.

Microhabitats

A microhabitat is a small home for plants and animals. It could be a pond, a tree, under a rock, or even a moldy apple! If it provides food, water, and shelter, animals can be found there.

Inside our bodies

The human body is an amazing machine, made up of many different parts. Each part does an important job, helping us think, feel, move, breathe, eat, and stay alive.

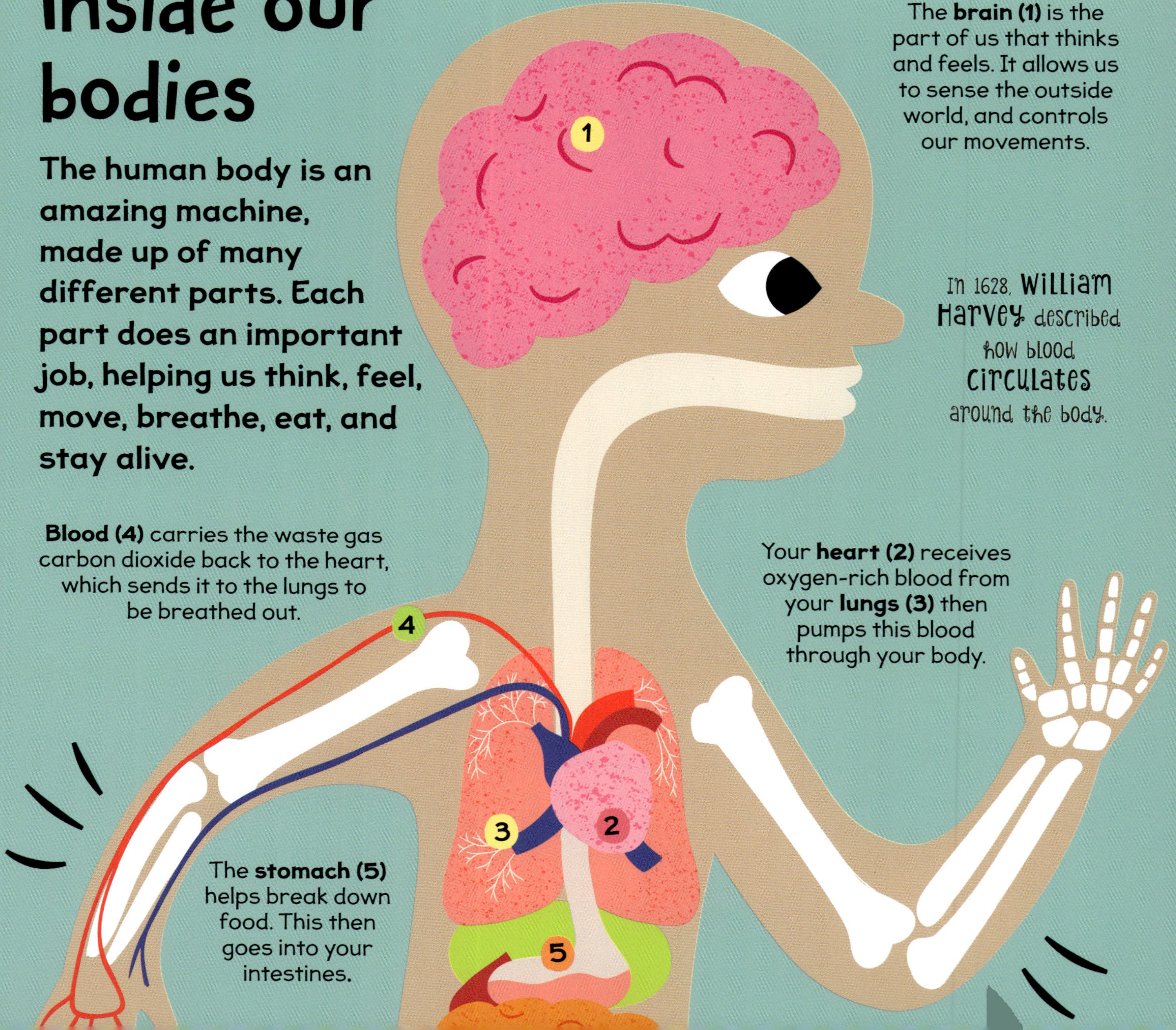

The **brain (1)** is the part of us that thinks and feels. It allows us to sense the outside world, and controls our movements.

In 1628, William Harvey described how blood circulates around the body.

Blood (4) carries the waste gas carbon dioxide back to the heart, which sends it to the lungs to be breathed out.

Your **heart (2)** receives oxygen-rich blood from your **lungs (3)** then pumps this blood through your body.

The **stomach (5)** helps break down food. This then goes into your intestines.

Skin (8) is the body's outer covering, protecting you from germs and injury.

Muscles (9) pull our bones so we can move.

Your **bladder (7)** stores urine, which you get rid of when you use the toilet.

In your **intestines (6)** food is broken down further. Useful substances are taken into the body through the intestine walls.

Bones (10) support the body and protect its organs.

Our skeleton is made up of more than 200 bones.

I CAN... TEST MY SENSES

Put on a blindfold. Ask a friend to choose some objects from around the house. Feel their shapes and textures. See if you can work out what they are.

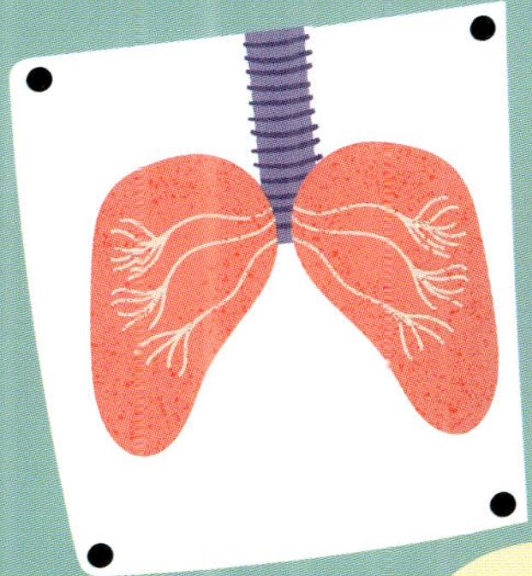

Keeping healthy

The best way of keeping healthy is with a healthy diet and regular exercise. Medical scientists study diseases and disorders of the human body and develop treatments for them.

I CAN... KEEP A FOOD DIARY

Why not track your eating habits by keeping a food diary. Write down everything you eat for a week. See if you can manage to keep a balanced diet.

My Meals

	Breakfast	Lunch	Dinner
Mon	cereal	Soup	Mac + cheese
Tue	oatmeal	Sandwich	Fish + veggie
Wed	Pancakes		
Thu			
Fri			
Sat			
Sun			

A balanced diet

A healthy diet is one that has a good balance of nutrients (substances that are good for us). The main nutrients found in food are proteins, carbohydrates, fats, and vitamins and minerals.

Happy minds

It's important to look after our minds, too. We can do this by talking about our feelings with friends and family, keeping active, being kind to others, and taking notice of the world around us.

Spending time outside helps you to relax. Have you been outside today?

Regular **exercise** is good for the heart, helps keep your body at a healthy weight, and lowers the risk of some diseases.

Sleep well

One of the best ways to look after ourselves is to have a good night's sleep. Our bodies need rest, too!

Rocky marvels

Rocks have an incredible history. As old as our planet, they are formed and shaped by fire, wind, water, and huge amounts of pressure.

1 Most rocks start as **igneous rock**, formed when hot, soft rock rises closer to Earth's surface, then cools and hardens.

I CAN... MAKE EDIBLE ROCK

Pour some brown and white chocolate chips into a glass. Crush the chips with a spoon. This is like sedimentary rock. Cover the glass and microwave for a few seconds. Now it's harder to see the different chips – like metamorphic rock.

2 Igneous rock slowly wears down into fragments called sediment. Over time the sediment forms **sedimentary rock**.

3 If igneous rock gets buried deeper in the Earth, heat and pressure bake it to form **metamorphic rock**.

Rock cycle

Rocks are constantly changing from one kind to another. This is called the rock cycle. We don't notice it because it happens over millions of years.

Volcanoes

The rocky layer that makes up Earth's surface is called the crust. Openings in the crust are called volcanoes. Gases, ash, and liquid rock from Earth's hot interior can burst out from a volcano.

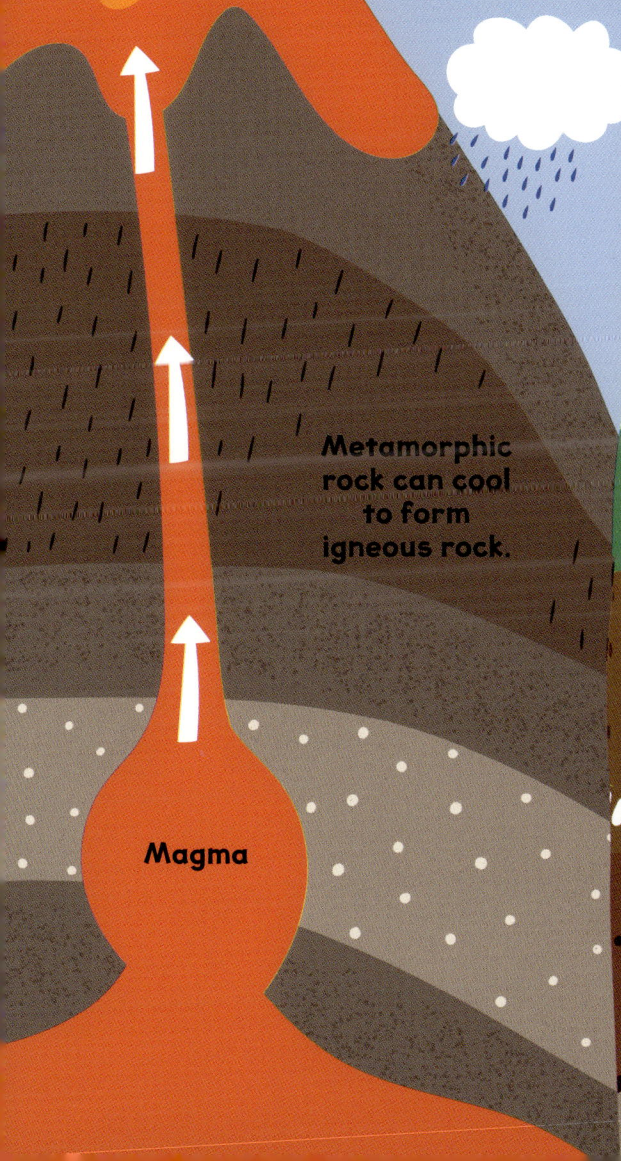

Life trapped in rocks

Some rocks contain fossils (preserved remains) of ancient creatures. Studying fossils teaches us about the history of life on our planet.

What is weather?

Scientists called meteorologists study the weather. They can predict the weather by looking at air temperature, air pressure, and the movement of water in the atmosphere.

I CAN... MAKE AN INDOOR RAINSTORM

Fill a glass halfway with warm water. Squirt some shaving cream on top. Add 20-30 drops of blue food coloring in the middle of the shaving cream. Wait for the blue "rain" to fall from the shaving cream "cloud."

The water cycle

Water is constantly moving through the atmosphere in a process called the water cycle. During the cycle, it takes different forms. When it's heated, it turns to a gas called vapor. When it cools, it turns to snow or hail.

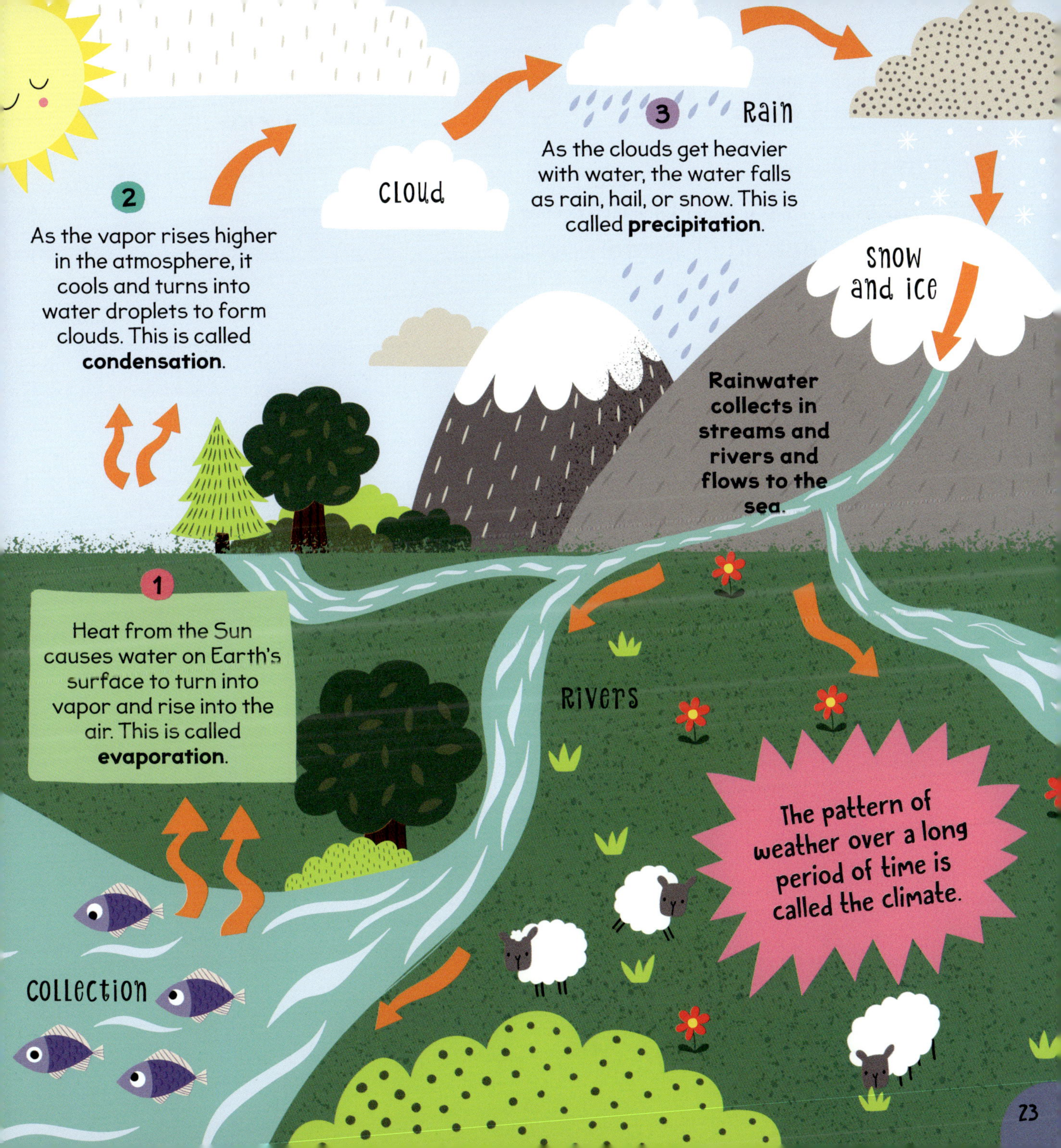
2
As the vapor rises higher in the atmosphere, it cools and turns into water droplets to form clouds. This is called **condensation**.
Cloud
3
Rain
As the clouds get heavier with water, the water falls as rain, hail, or snow. This is called **precipitation**.
Snow and ice
Rainwater collects in streams and rivers and flows to the sea.
1
Heat from the Sun causes water on Earth's surface to turn into vapor and rise into the air. This is called **evaporation**.
Rivers
The pattern of weather over a long period of time is called the climate.
Collection

Seasons

Each year our planet goes through four seasons: spring, summer, autumn, and winter. The weather changes in each season, and plants and animals find ways to adapt.

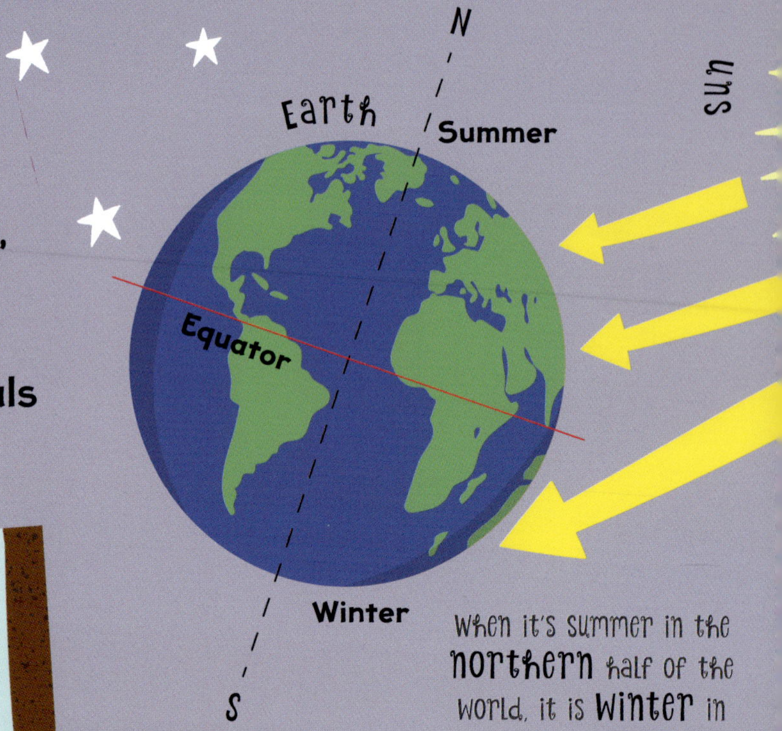

When it's summer in the **northern** half of the world, it is **winter** in the **south**.

Spring

The weather turns warmer and days grow longer. Plants begin to flower and animals produce their young.

Summer

Days are long and sunny. Trees have full green leaves and produce fruit, and flowers bloom.

On a tilt

We have seasons because Earth is tilted as it orbits (travels around) the Sun. So different parts receive more or less sunlight at different times of the year.

I CAN... MAKE A SEASONS POSTER

Take a big piece of paper and divide it into four sections. Title them Spring, Summer, Autumn, and Winter. Draw an oak tree in each box to show how it changes from season to season.

Autumn

The weather turns cooler and the days grow shorter. Leaves turn brown and yellow, and animals grow thicker coats.

For countries near the equator, there are only two seasons - wet and dry.

Winter

The weather turns cold. Many trees lose their leaves and plants stop growing. Some animals travel to warmer places or go into a deep sleep.

Many animals sleep more in winter.

Spectacular space

Throughout history, people have wondered about the stars in the night sky. Today, we have powerful telescopes that enable us to see further than ever before.

Our star

The Sun is our nearest star and provides us with warmth and light. It is 93 million miles away from Earth.

The Sun is around 4.6 billion years old.

The **Moon** is Earth's only natural satellite. It is 238,900 miles away and orbits our planet once every 27 days.

Our solar family

Earth is one of eight planets in orbit around the Sun. Together they form the Solar System, which also includes asteroids, comets, moons, and dwarf planets, such as Pluto.

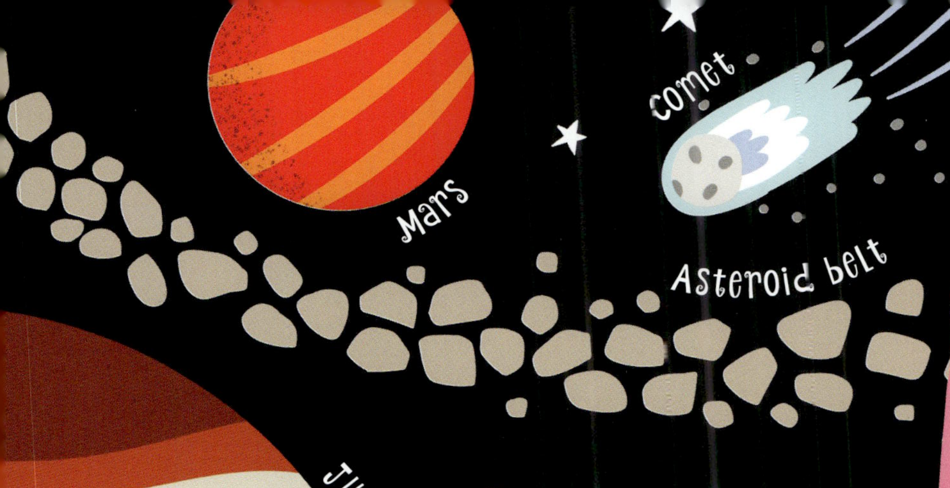

I CAN... MAKE MOON CRATERS

The Moon is covered with craters caused by the impact of rocks from space. Add a thick layer of flour to a pan. Drop pebbles in to make craters.

The Milky Way

Our Solar System is part of a galaxy (a giant cluster of stars) called the Milky Way, which is made up of around 100 billion stars, many of which have their own solar systems.

Useful materials

Everything around us is made from materials, from clothes to toys. Scientists study materials and try to develop new ones that may be useful. Each material has certain properties.

1 **Plastics** are mainly made from chemicals and are not found in nature. They are waterproof, light, strong, and easy to make.

2 **Wood** is strong, flexible, and long-lasting. It is used to make furniture and the frames of houses.

3 **Metals** are strong, hard, shiny materials. They are used to make cutlery, coins, cars, and planes.

Natural rubber is a super-stretchy material that comes from the rubber tree.

Fabrics are soft, smooth and flexible. Clothing, bags, curtains, and towels are all made of different kinds of fabric.

Glass is usually see-through, so it is good for windows and glasses. Thick glass is strong, but thin glass breaks easily.

I CAN... GUESS THE MATERIAL

Find ten household objects and group them according to their material. Think about why they are made of that material and not another.

Fascinating forces

A force can make an object change its shape or the way it moves. Forces can squeeze or stretch an object. They can make it go faster, or slow it down.

Gravity keeps Earth in orbit around the Sun, and stops us from falling off!

1 On a roller coaster, a car is pulled down a slope by gravity.

2 The car gathers enough speed to climb up the next slope.

Gravity

The force that attracts objects towards each other is called gravity. The bigger the object, the greater its gravitational pull.

Tension

As a swing ride rotates at speed, tension in the chain causes the swing to fly out.

Friction

When two surfaces slide past each other on a roller coaster or ride, a force called friction is produced. This slows down or stops a moving object.

I CAN... TEST FRICTION

Try rolling a toy car across different surfaces – carpet and laminate floor (or metal tray). Which one gives the the smoothest ride? What does this tell us about the force of friction?

Machine power

We all use machines. They can be very complex, but simple machines have been around for centuries. Machines reduce the amount of effort needed to perform tasks, such as moving heavy objects.

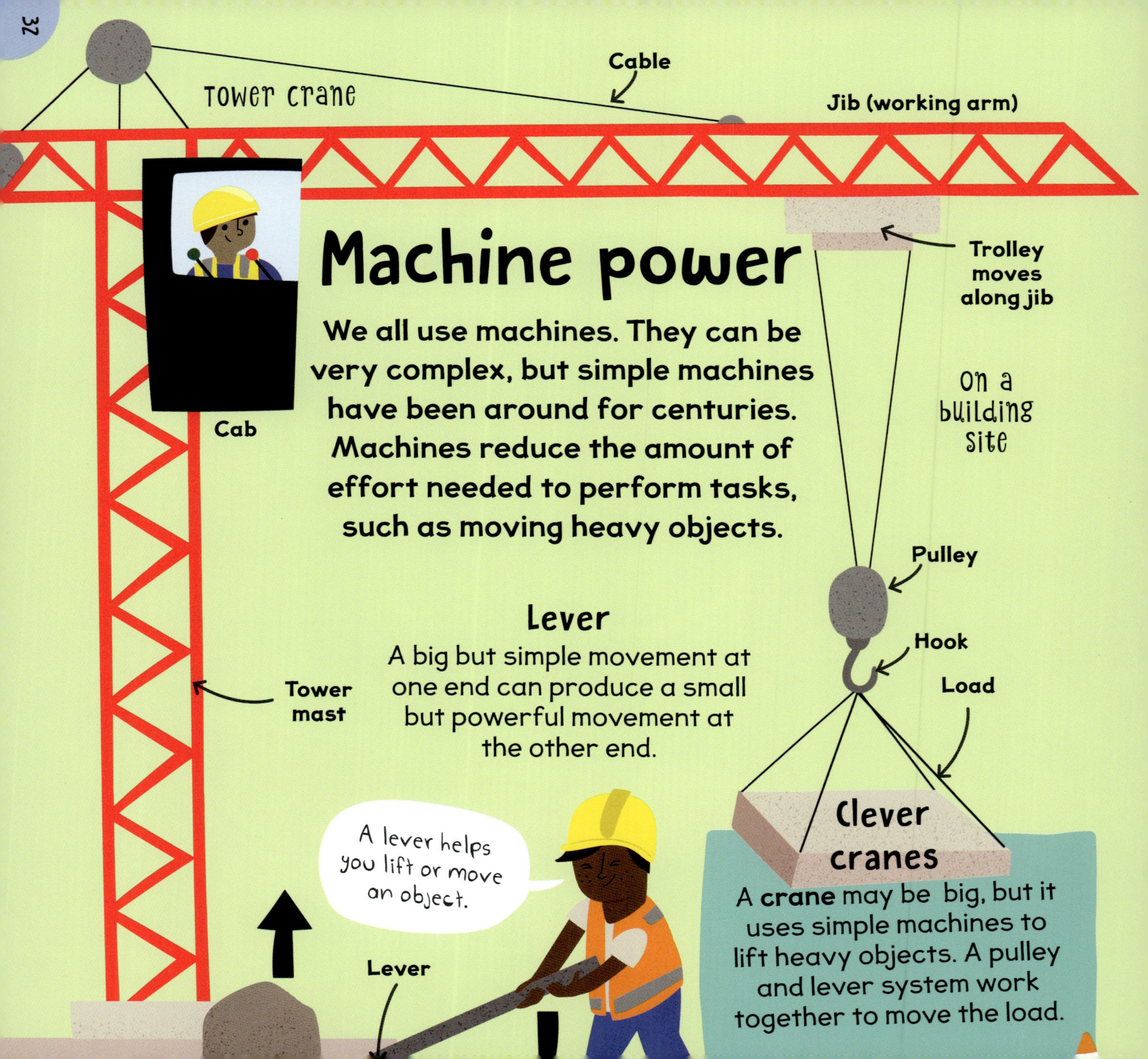

Lever

A big but simple movement at one end can produce a small but powerful movement at the other end.

Clever cranes

A **crane** may be big, but it uses simple machines to lift heavy objects. A pulley and lever system work together to move the load.

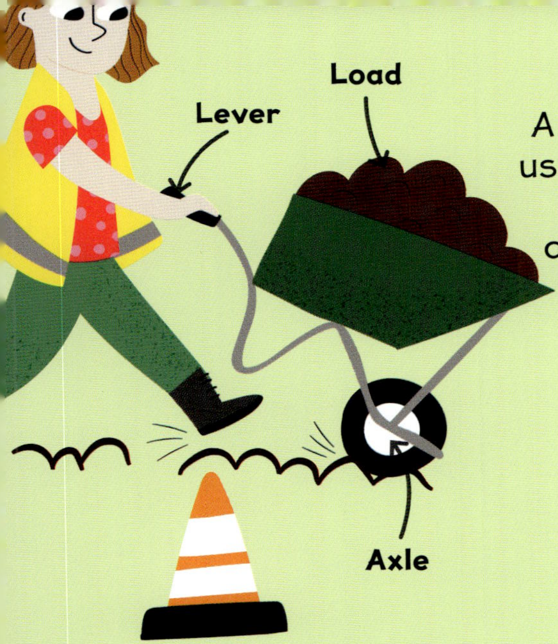

Wheel and axle

A **wheelbarrow** is a very useful simple machine. The wheel, axle, and lever allow heavy loads to be moved around easily.

Inclined plane

This is a sloping surface that is used to move heavy objects. It is helpful because it takes less effort to slide an object up a slope than to lift it.

I CAN... MAKE A CARDBOARD TUBE CAR

You can make a wheel and axle machine in the form of a car. Use a toilet roll tube, straws for axles, and plastic bottle caps for wheels.

Super spiral

A **screw** is a cylinder with a spiral groove running up its length. It can be used to lift things or hold them together.

Looking at light

Light is a form of energy that our eyes can detect. The Sun is the main source of light on Earth. Most light comes from heat. When something gets very hot, it often gives off light.

In space, light travels extremely fast, at 186,000 miles a second.

We see an object when light reflects off it and into our eye.

Refraction

Light can pass through transparent materials, like glass and water, but they cause the light to bend. This is called refraction.

Reflection

When light hits a smooth, shiny surface that it can't pass through, such as a mirror, it bounces off in a different direction. This is called reflection.

Refraction makes the duck's body look as if it is cut in half.

Fireflies aren't hot!

Not all light is hot, and not all hot things give off light. The light made by fireflies isn't hot, and radiators do not give off light.

We see **lightning** before we hear **thunder** because **light** travels **faster** than **sound**.

Light travels in straight lines – it can't bend around things.

Shadows

A shadow is a dark shape caused by an object blocking a source of light. The shadow's outline is the same shape as the object blocking the light.

I CAN... MAKE SHADOW PUPPETS

All you need are your hands, a wall, and a bedside lamp or table lamp. Put one hand between the light and the wall so that you can clearly see the shadow of your hand. By changing the shape of your hand, you can make animals, birds, and other characters.

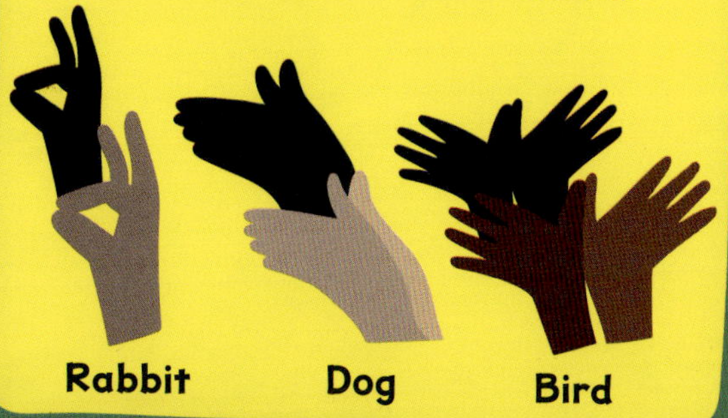

Color

Light looks white, but it's actually made up of different colors. Our eyes can detect three colors: red, green, and blue. These are the primary colors. By combining them, we can see many other colors.

The word orange comes from the fruit, not the color. The word for the color used to be geoluread.

Butterflies can see many more colors than humans can.

Rainbows

When sunlight passes through raindrops, the light splits into its different colors and spreads across the sky.

The seven colors of the rainbow are: red, orange, yellow, green, blue, indigo, and violet.

Colors in the wild

Animals use colors in lots of ways: to attract a mate, to warn off rivals, or for disguise to avoid predators. Chameleons can change color to communicate with other chameleons.

The color of objects

Objects absorb and reflect light differently. A tomato reflects red light and absorbs all the other colors, so only the red light is seen by our eyes.

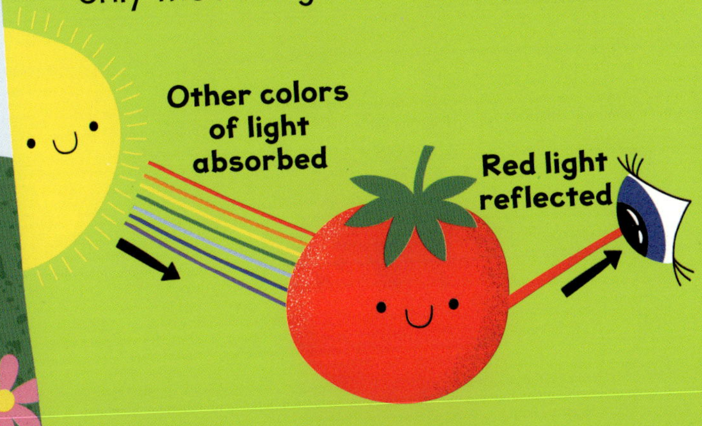

I CAN... MIX COLORS

Fill two bottles with water. Add blue food coloring to one, and yellow to the other. Pour some of both into a plastic bowl. What color do you get?

Sounds good!

Sound happens when something vibrates. The vibration moves through the air as energy called sound waves. Our ears collect sounds and our brain tells us what they are. Talking, music, and thunder are types of sound.

If you scream in space, it makes no sound as there is no air.

We measure the loudness of sound in decibels.

Jet plane taking off
140 decibels

Thunderclap
120 decibels

Helicopter
100 decibels

Train
80 decibels

Talking
60 decibels

Birdsong
40 decibels

Rustling leaves
20 decibels

Breathing
10 decibels

Sounds are loud or soft depending on the strength of the vibrations.

The stronger the vibrations, the louder the sound.

High and low

The pitch of a sound is how high or low it is. This depends on the speed of the vibrations. Quick vibrations produce high-pitched sounds. Slow vibrations produce low-pitched sounds.

Carrying sounds

Sound waves need a medium, like air or water, to carry them. Sound is also carried through solids like iron, wood, and stone. It travels faster through these denser substances.

I CAN... MAKE A CUP-AND-STRING PHONE

Connect two paper cups with a long piece of string. Take turns with your friends to talk and listen through the "phone." Sound waves travel along the string to the cup at the other end.

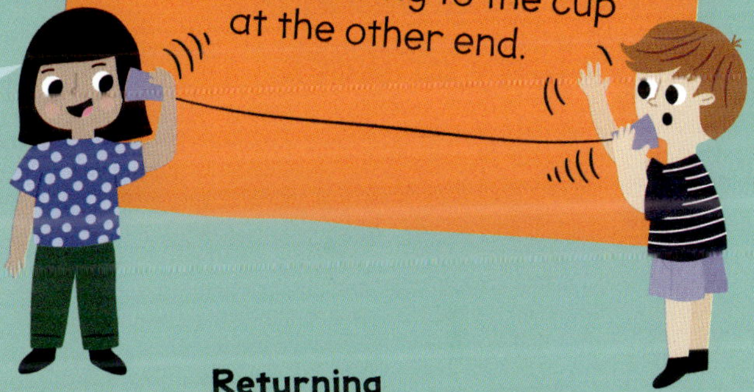

When sound waves bounce off smooth, hard surfaces, they reflect back as echoes.

Underwater echoes

Dolphins make loud clicks and squeals to help them find food. The sounds bounce back off nearby prey, helping the dolphins locate it. This is called echolocation.

All electric

Electricity is a form of energy. It is caused by the flow of tiny particles called electrons. We use electricity in our homes to power our appliances. It can also be found in nature – lightning is electricity at work.

How it's made

Electricity is generated in power stations, then sent through cables to our homes. It can be made by burning coal, oil, and gas (fossil fuels). But the best way to make it is by using the natural powers of sunlight, sea, and wind.

Electric circuit

An electric current is the flow of electrons along a loop of wire, called a circuit. This can be used to power a device such as a light. You can break the circuit with a switch, stopping the electricity from flowing.

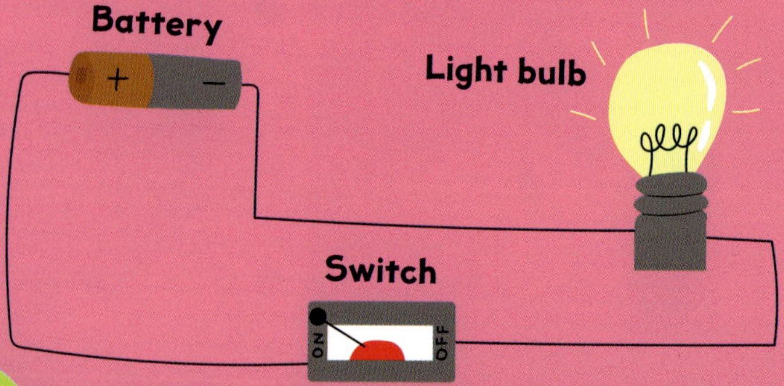

How to use less

We can save electricity by turning off lights and appliances when not in use, and by using energy-saving light bulbs.

I CAN... MAKE STATIC ELECTRICITY

If you rub a balloon against your sweater, it knocks electrons from atoms in the sweater onto the balloon. Does the balloon stick to you? This is static electricity.

Mega magnets

Magnetism is an invisible force that certain objects have. It causes them to attract (pull closer) or repel (push away) other objects. Magnetic objects contain metal, such as iron or nickel.

I CAN... MAKE A FLOATING COMPASS

Magnetize a needle by stroking it with a magnet. Then put it on top of a disc of cork. Place on a dish of water. The needle will turn and point north.

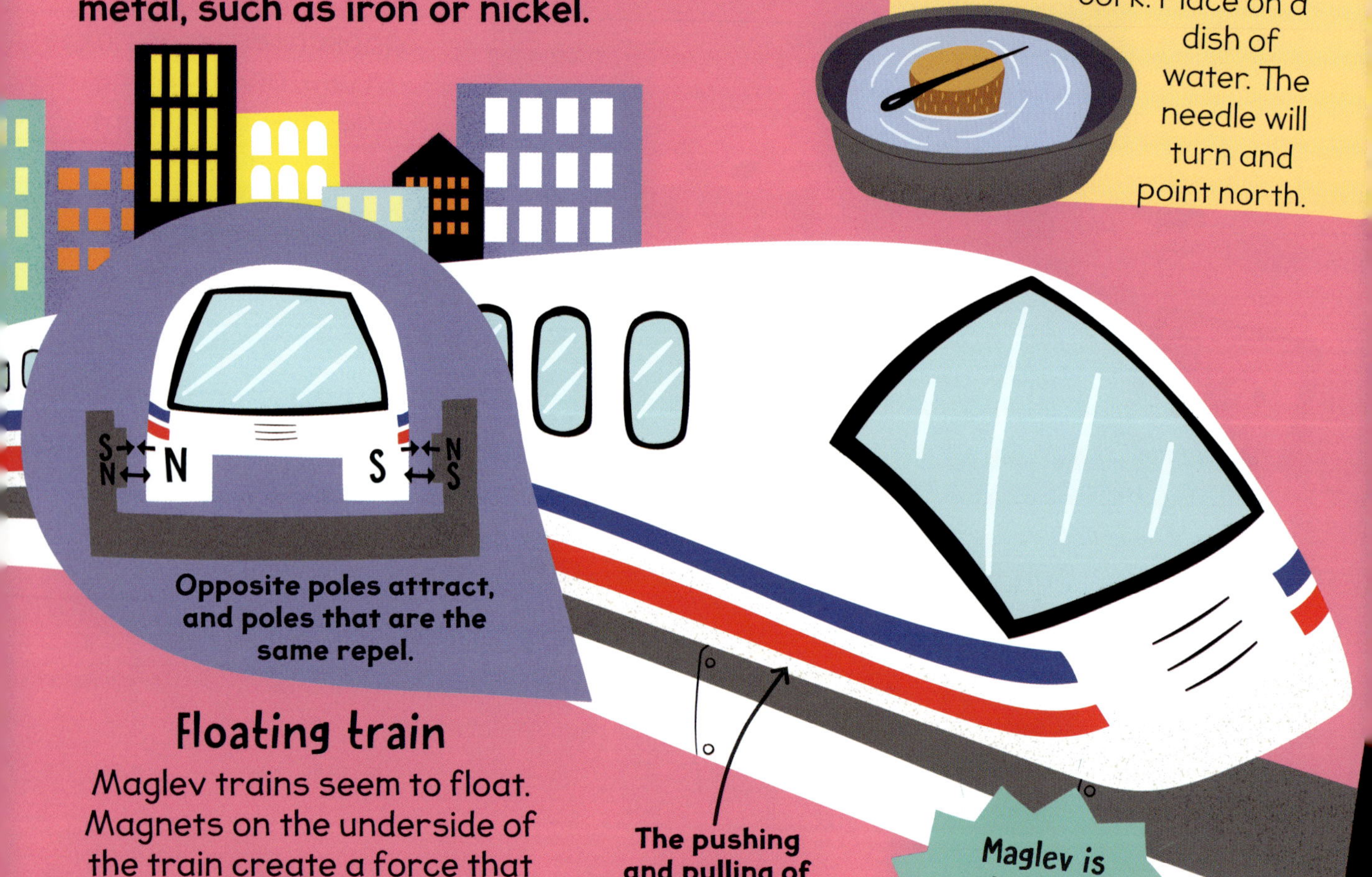

Opposite poles attract, and poles that are the same repel.

The pushing and pulling of magnets help to raise the train from the track

Floating train

Maglev trains seem to float. Magnets on the underside of the train create a force that either attracts or repels against magnets on the track.

Maglev is short for magnetic levitation.

Magnetic fields

A magnet's magnetic force flows from the north pole to the south pole. The area around a magnet affected by this force is called its magnetic field.

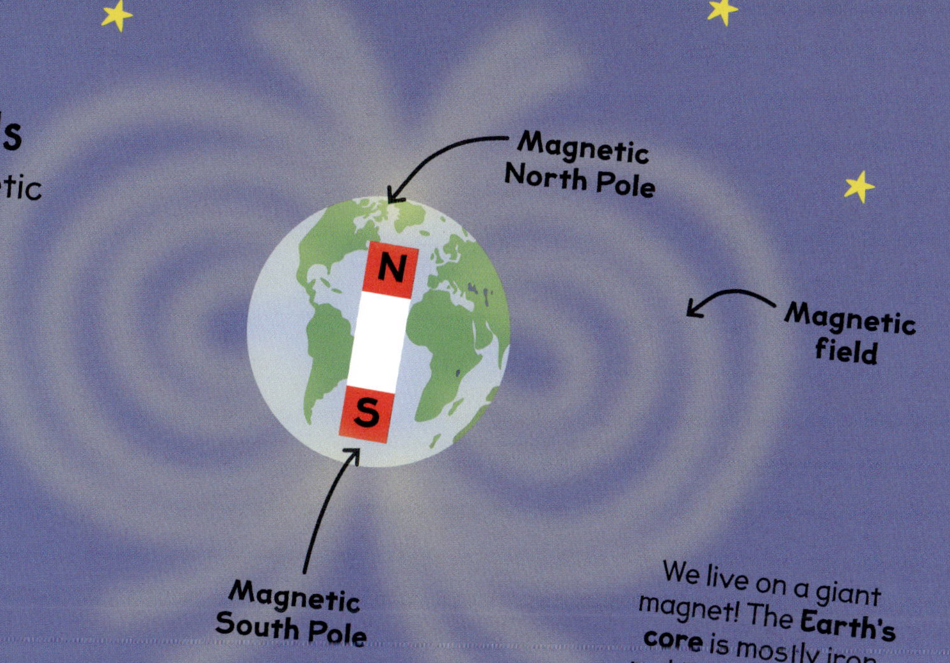

We live on a giant magnet! The **Earth's core** is mostly iron, making Earth a giant magnet, with its own North and South Poles.

Super science!

Scientists help us to understand the world and the Universe. For centuries, people have asked questions and tested their theories.

Climate change

Scientists have identified the threat of climate change and showed us ways of improving the environment through cleaner forms of energy.

Solar panels capture the Sun's energy.

Technology

Scientists' study of matter, energy, forces, electricity, and magnetism have helped us build technologies we rely on. Phones, cars, computers, and the Internet would not exist without the work of scientists.

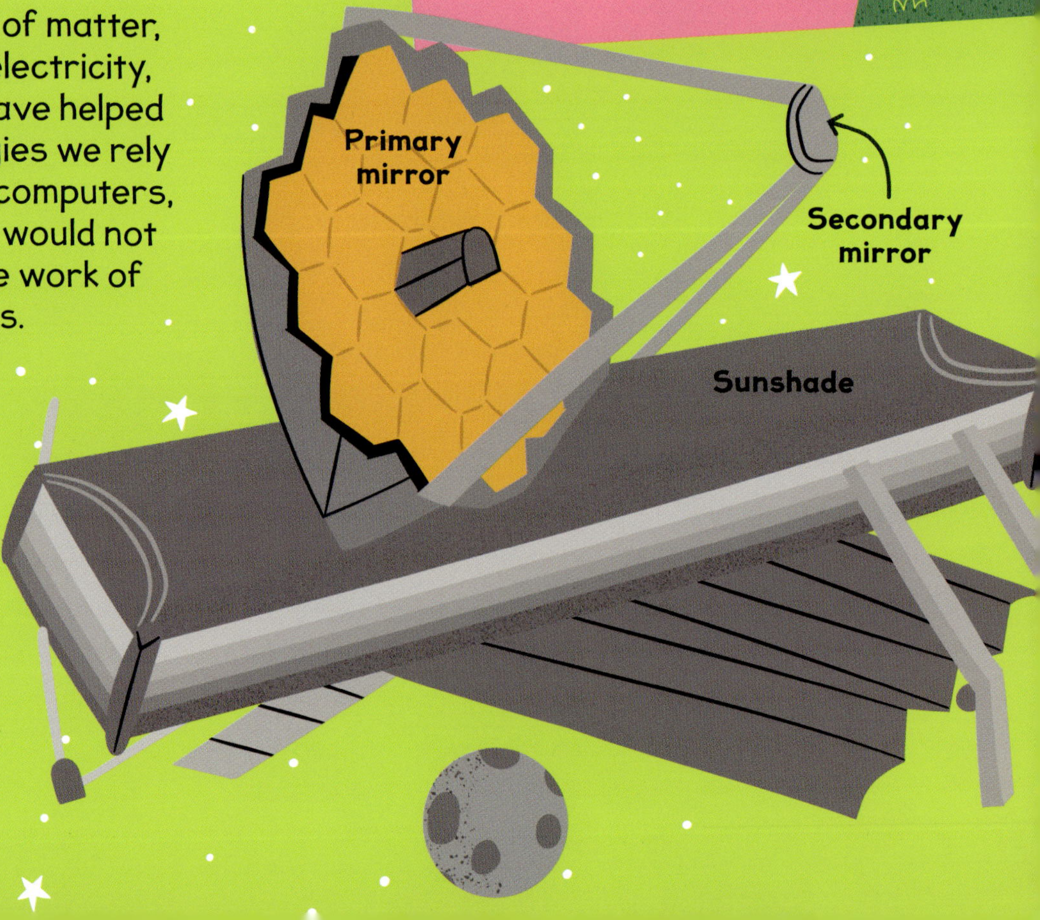

The **James Webb Space Telescope** is the most powerful telescope ever built. It was launched into space in 2021.

Wind turbines harness the power of the wind to make electricity.

Hydropower uses running water to help make electricity.

It usually takes years to develop a vaccine. The first vaccines for COVID-19 were rolled out in just 11 months.

Vaccines

Scientists have developed vaccines in the fight against disease. Vaccines make our bodies stronger so they can fight off tiny germs called viruses. COVID-19 is an example of a virus.

I CAN... MAKE A POSTER

Create a poster showing different ways we can help our planet by saving energy. Investigate other simple things you can do to cut back on energy use at home.

The study of the human body has given us more knowledge about how to lead healthy lives.

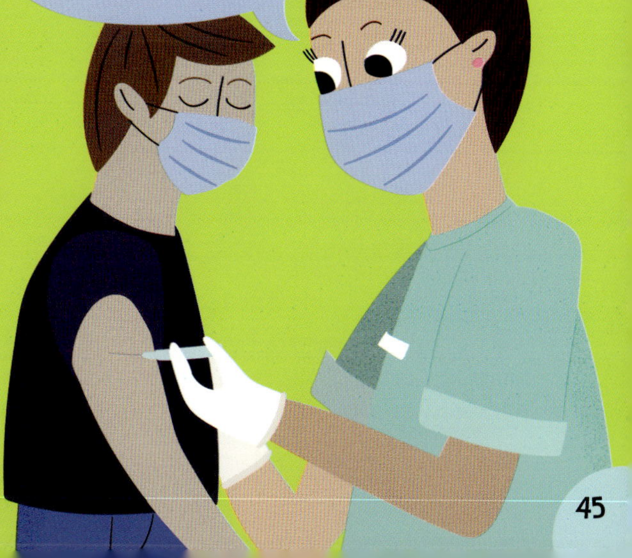

Cool scientists!

Here are some incredible scientists, past and present. Some have helped to change our understanding of the world, while others have inspired us to find out more about science. Could you become one of them?

Yes, you could!

Maggie Aderin-Pocock

1968

Space scientist and communicator Maggie Aderin-Pocock is inspiring thousands of young people to be the next generation of scientists.

Mary Anning

1799-1847

Mary was just 12 when she found a fossilized ichthyosaur skeleton. She found many fossils, and encouraged the study of ancient creatures.

David Attenborough

1926

Sir David Attenborough is a passionate campaigner for the environment. His wildlife documentaries have been watched by millions around the world.

Rachel Carson

1907-1964

A marine biologist, conservationist, and author, Rachel Carson's books inspired people to start thinking about and caring for the environment.

Marie Curie

1867-1934

In 1903, Marie Curie became the first woman to be awarded a Nobel Prize (for physics). She was awarded it again in 1911, for chemistry.

Charles Darwin

1809-1882

In 1859, Darwin's theory of evolution was published in his book *On the Origin of Species*. He is one of the most important scientists in history.

Albert Einstein

1879-1955

One of the greatest physicists of all time, Einstein's theory of special relativity overturned our understanding of the nature of time and space.

Rosalind Franklin

1920–1958

In 1952, Rosalind Franklin's X-ray photograph helped to reveal the twisted, ladderlike structure of human DNA, found in all our cells.

Jane Goodall

1934

Jane Goodall is a world expert on chimpanzees. She works hard to encourage conservation to help heal the damage humans have done to the planet.

Stephen Hawking

1942–2018

Our understanding of the Universe was changed by Stephen Hawking's work on black holes. His book *A Brief History of Time* was a worldwide bestseller.

Isaac Newton

1642–1727

Famous for his theory of gravity in 1666, Newton also discovered that every object in the Universe obeys three laws of motion.